Piano Solo

THE WORLD'S GREAT CLAS

Easier Piano Classics

89 Original Works by 28 Great Composers

Easy to Intermediate Piano Solos

EDITED BY MARGARET OTWELL AND RICHARD WALTERS

MARK CARLSTEIN, ASSISTANT EDITOR

Cover Painting: Berckheyde, *The Smedestraat*, 1680

ISBN 978-0-634-01266-2

HAL•LEONARD®
CORPORATION
7777 W. BLUEMOUND RD. P.O. BOX 13819 MILWAUKEE, WI 53213

Visit Hal Leonard Online at
www.halleonard.com

CONTENTS

4

Capriccio

Carl Philipp Emanuel Bach
1714–1788

Invention No. 13 in A Minor

Johann Sebastian Bach
1685–1750

Gavotte
from FRENCH SUITE NO. 5

Johann Sebastian Bach
1685–1750
BWV 816

[Allegro]

Giguetta

Johann Sebastian Bach
1685–1750

Invention No. 14 in B-flat Major

Johann Sebastian Bach
1685–1750

[Andante con moto]

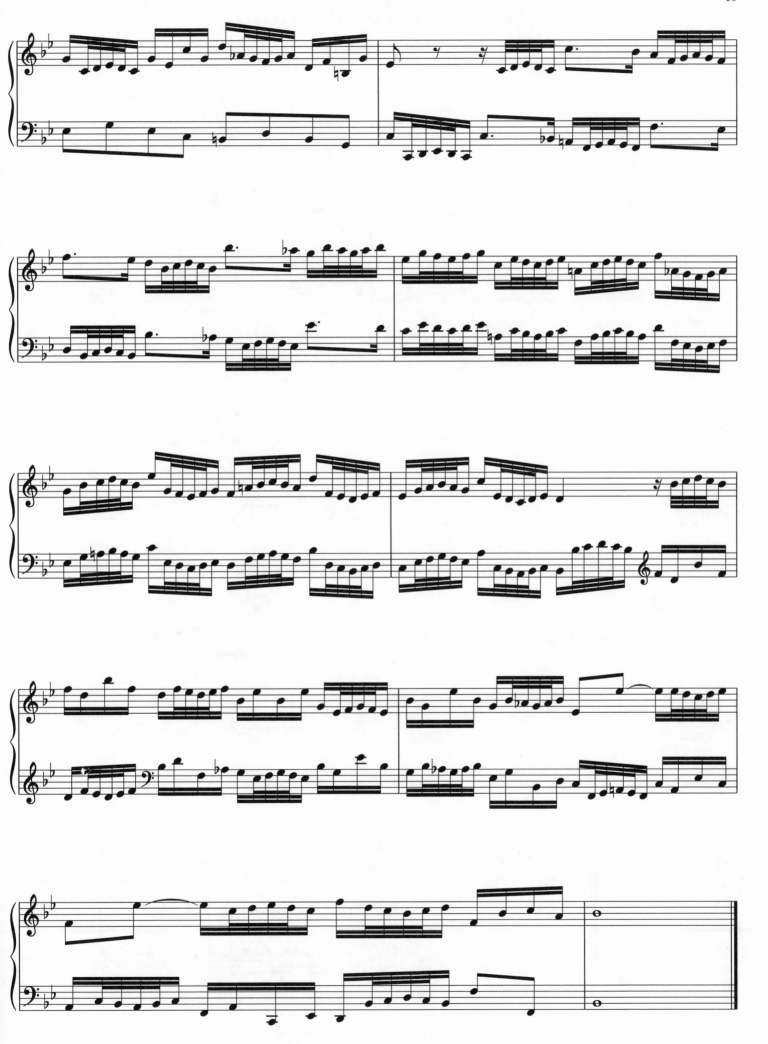

March in E-flat Major

Johann Sebastian Bach
1685–1750

[Allegro moderato]

[*mf*]

Sarabande
from FRENCH SUITE No. 3

Johann Sebastian Bach
1685–1750
BWV 814

Bagatelle

Ludwig van Beethoven
1770–1827
Op. 33, No. 3

Bagatelle

Ludwig van Beethoven
1770–1827
Op. 119, No. 1

Bagatelle

Ludwig van Beethoven
1770–1827
Op. 119, No. 4

Country Dance No. 1

Ludwig van Beethoven
1770–1827

Sonatina in F Major

Ludwig van Beethoven
1770–1827

Rondo

Allegro

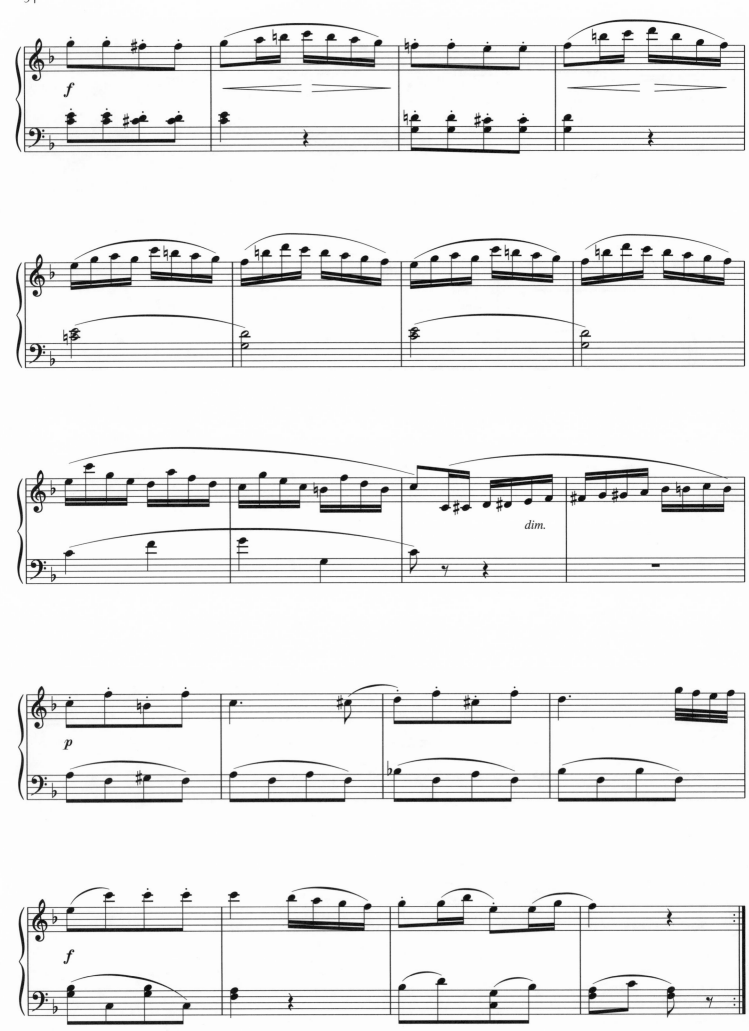

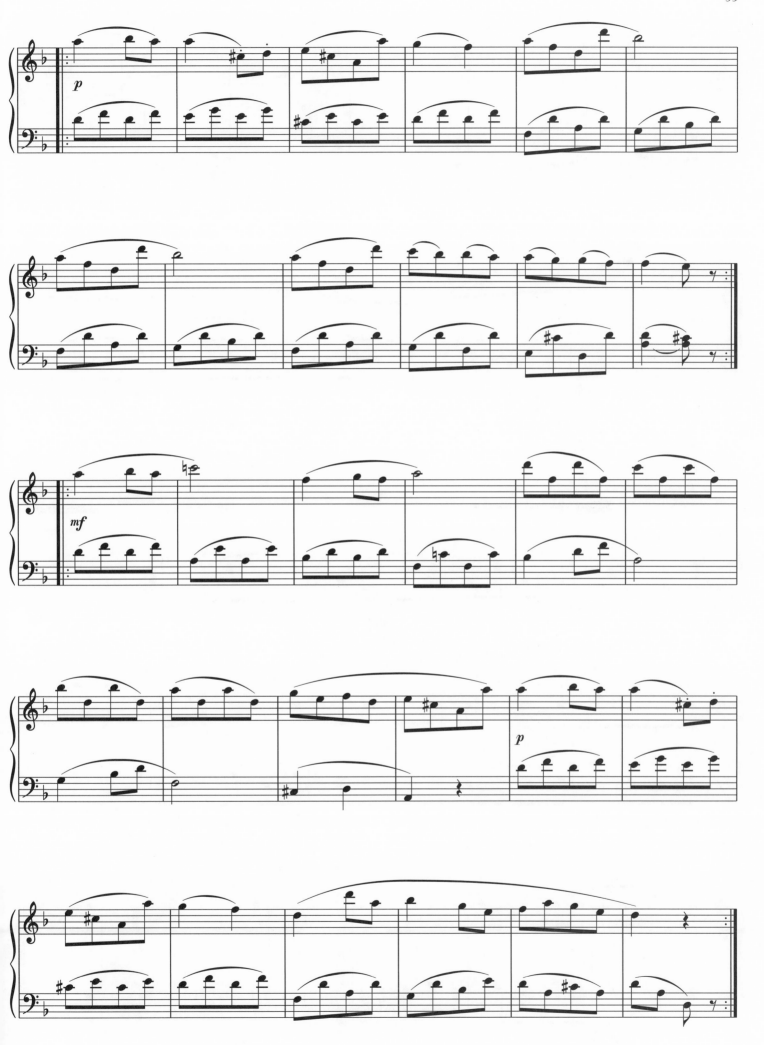

Variations on a Swiss Song

Ludwig van Beethoven
1770–1827
WoO 64

Theme

Andante con moto

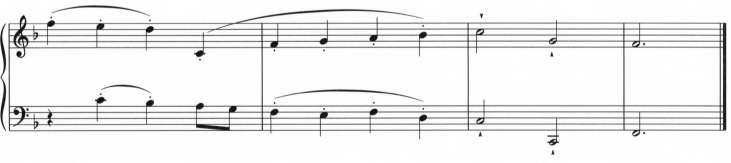

Var. I

Var. II

Var. III

Minore

sempre piano e legato

Var. IV

Maggiore

f

Var. V

sempre dolce

Var. VI

Sonatina in G Major

Ludwig van Beethoven
1770–1827

44

Romanza
Allegretto

Courante

John Blow
1648–1708

[Moderato]

[mf]

Prelude

John Blow
1648–1708

[Allegro]

[mf]

Ave Maria

Johann Friedrich Burgmüller
1806–1874
Op. 100, No. 19

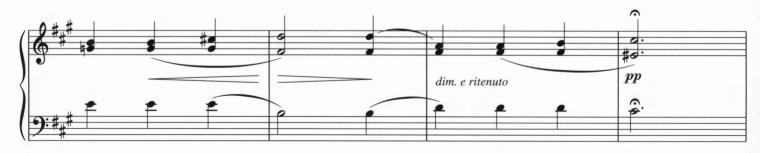

Ballade

Johann Friedrich Burgmüller
1806–1874
Op. 100, No. 15

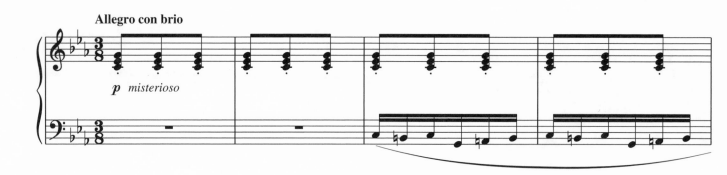

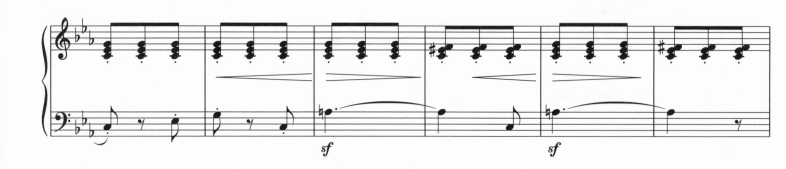

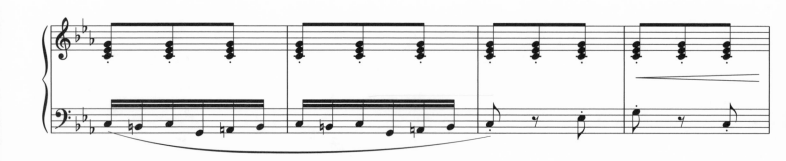

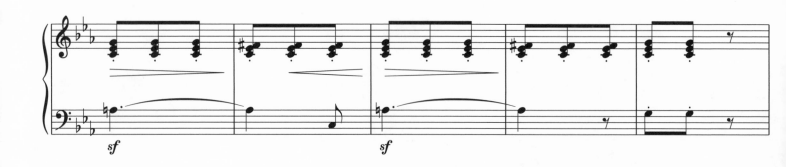

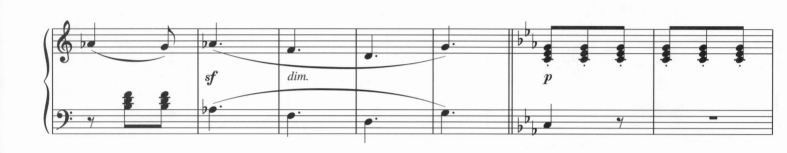

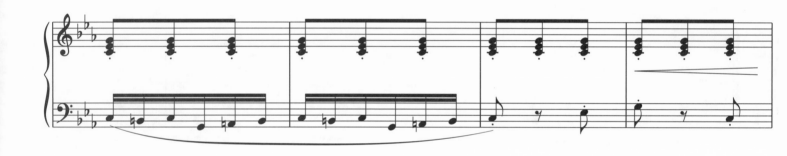

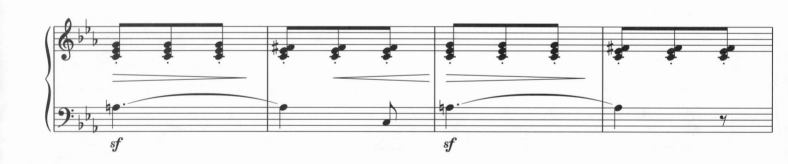

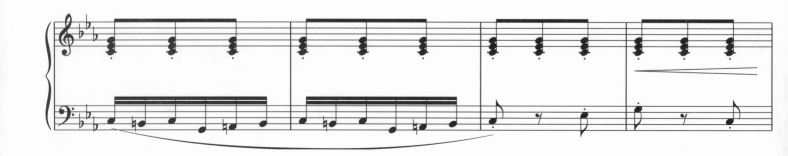

The Chase

Johann Friedrich Burgmüller
1806–1874
Op. 100, No. 9

Allegro vivace

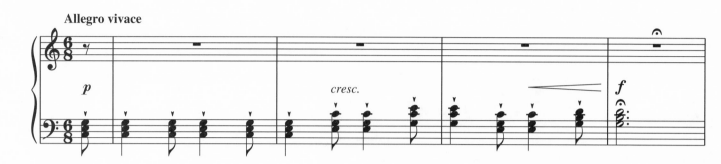

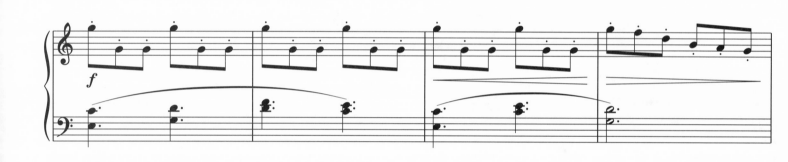

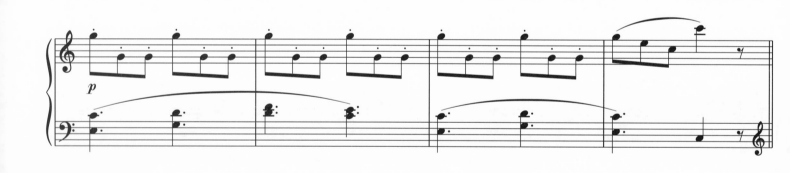

un poco agitato

Tarantella

Johann Friedrich Burgmüller
1806–1874
Op. 100, No. 20

Harmony of the Angels

Johann Friedrich Burgmüller
1806–1874
Op. 100, No. 21

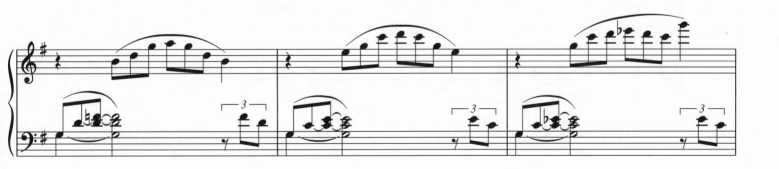

The Return

Johann Friedrich Burgmüller
1806–1874
Op. 100, No. 23

Molto agitato, quasi presto

Mazurka in E Minor

Fryderyk Chopin
1810–1849
Op. 17, No. 2

67

Mazurka in F Major

Fryderyk Chopin
1810–1849
Op. 68, No. 3 (Posthumous)

Mazurka in G Minor

Fryderyk Chopin
1810–1849
Op. 67, No. 2 (Posthumous)

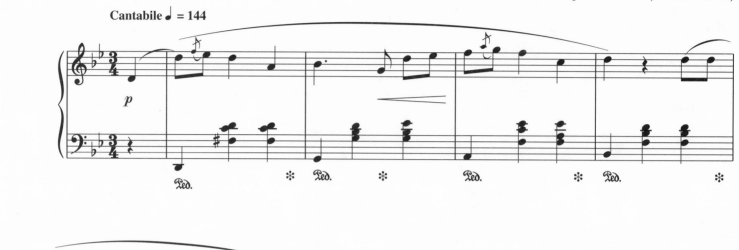

Polonaise in G Minor

Fryderyk Chopin
1810–1849
Op. Posthumous

Polonaise da capo al fine

Nocturne in C-sharp Minor

Fryderyk Chopin
1810–1849
Op. Posthumous

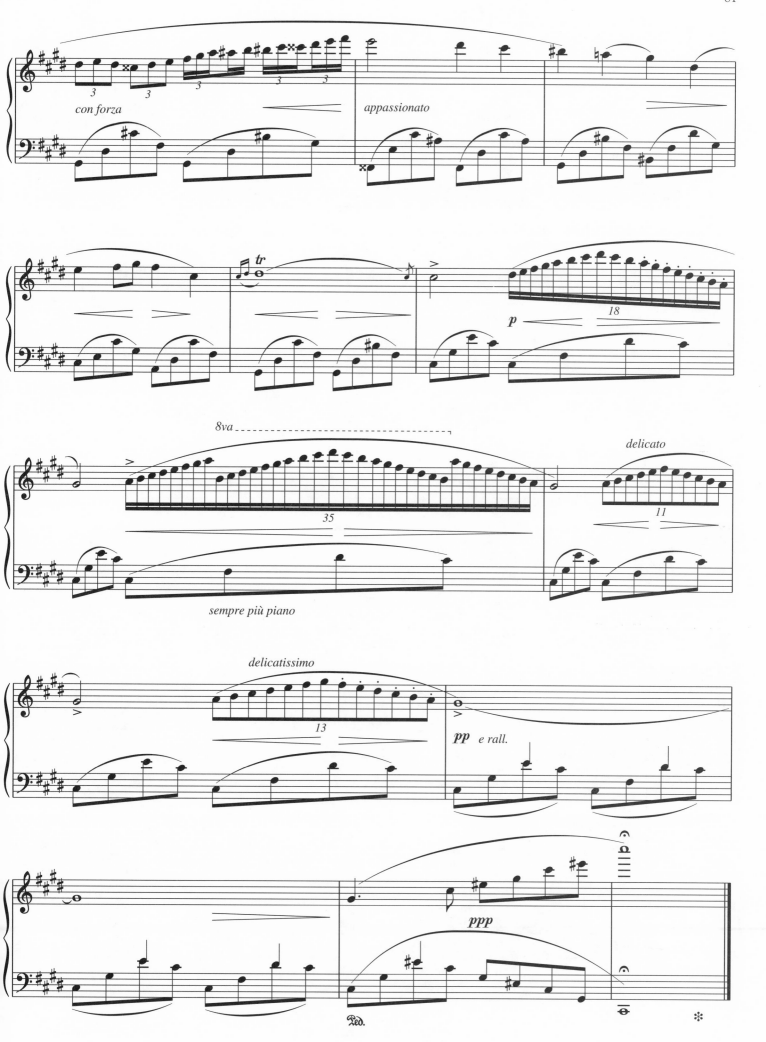

Nocturne in G Minor

Fryderyk Chopin
1810–1849
Op. 15, No. 3

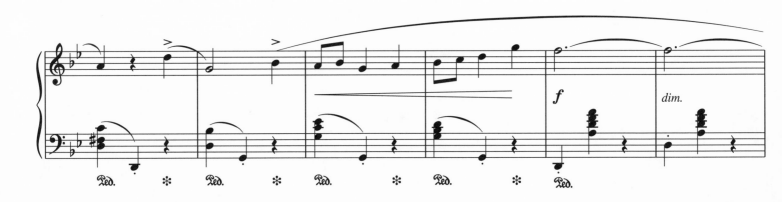

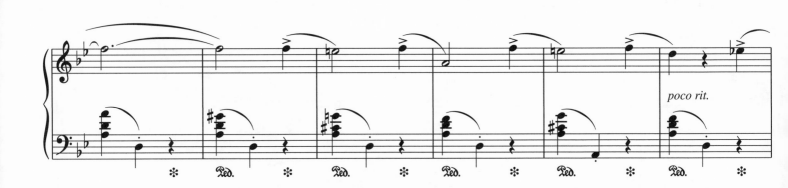

Waltz in B Minor

Fryderyk Chopin
1810–1849
Op. 69, No. 2 (Posthumous)

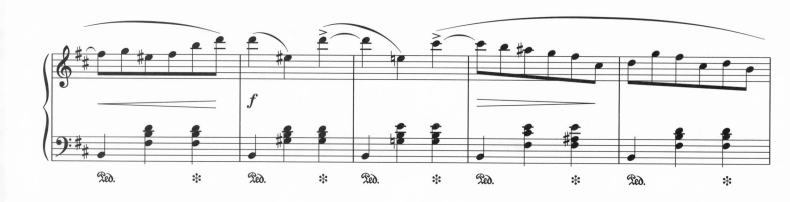

Waltz in F Minor

Fryderyk Chopin
1810–1849
Op. 70, No. 2

Monferrina in C Major

Muzio Clementi
1752–1832
WO 15

Allegro con brio

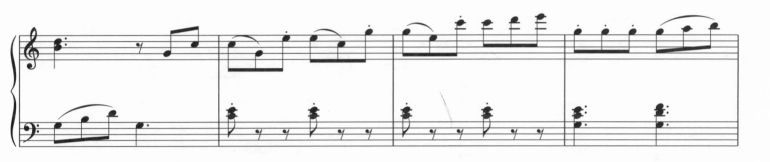

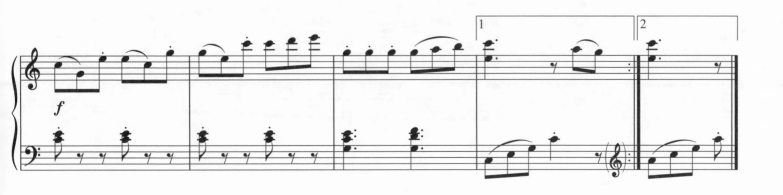

Gavotta

Arcangelo Corelli
1653–1713

Moderato

Le Coucou

Louis-Claude Daquin
1694–1772

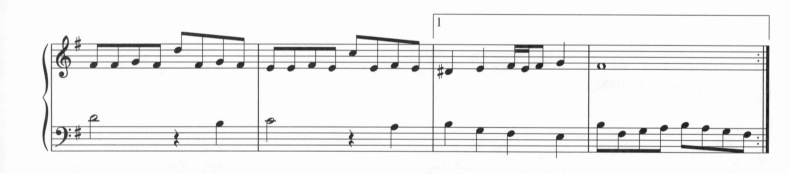

D.C. al Coda
(with repeats)

CODA

O, My Charmer, Spare Me

Louis Moreau Gottschalk
1829–1869

107

Arietta
from LYRIC PIECES, BOOK 1

Edvard Grieg
1843–1907
Op. 12, No. 1

Poco andante e sostenuto

Folksong
from LYRIC PIECES, BOOK 1

Edvard Grieg
1843–1907
Op. 12, No. 5

Con moto

Folksong
from LYRIC PIECES, BOOK 2

Edvard Grieg
1843–1907
Op. 38, No. 2

Watchman's Song
from LYRIC PIECES, BOOK 1

Edvard Grieg
1843–1907
Op. 12, No. 3

INTERMEZZO
Spirit of the Night

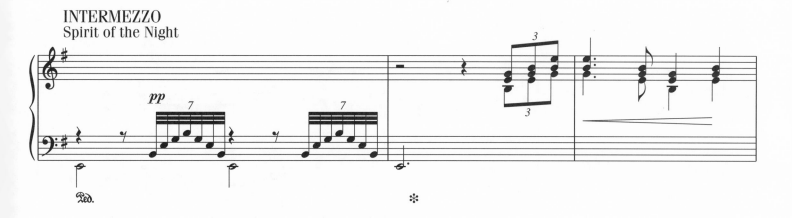

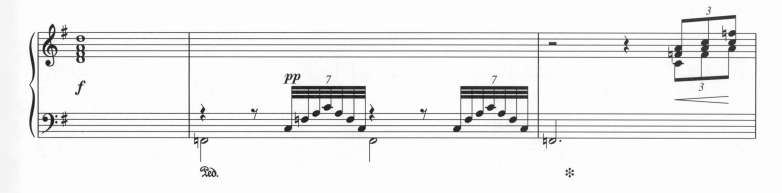

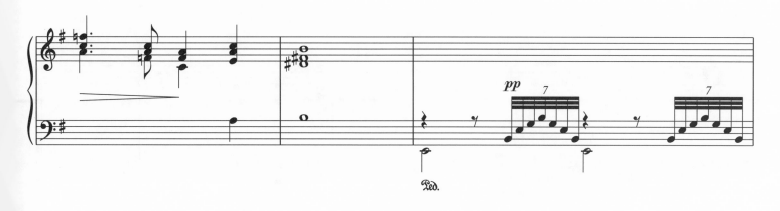

The Fair
from ALBUMLEAVES FOR THE YOUNG

Cornelius Gurlitt
1820–1901
Op. 101, No. 8

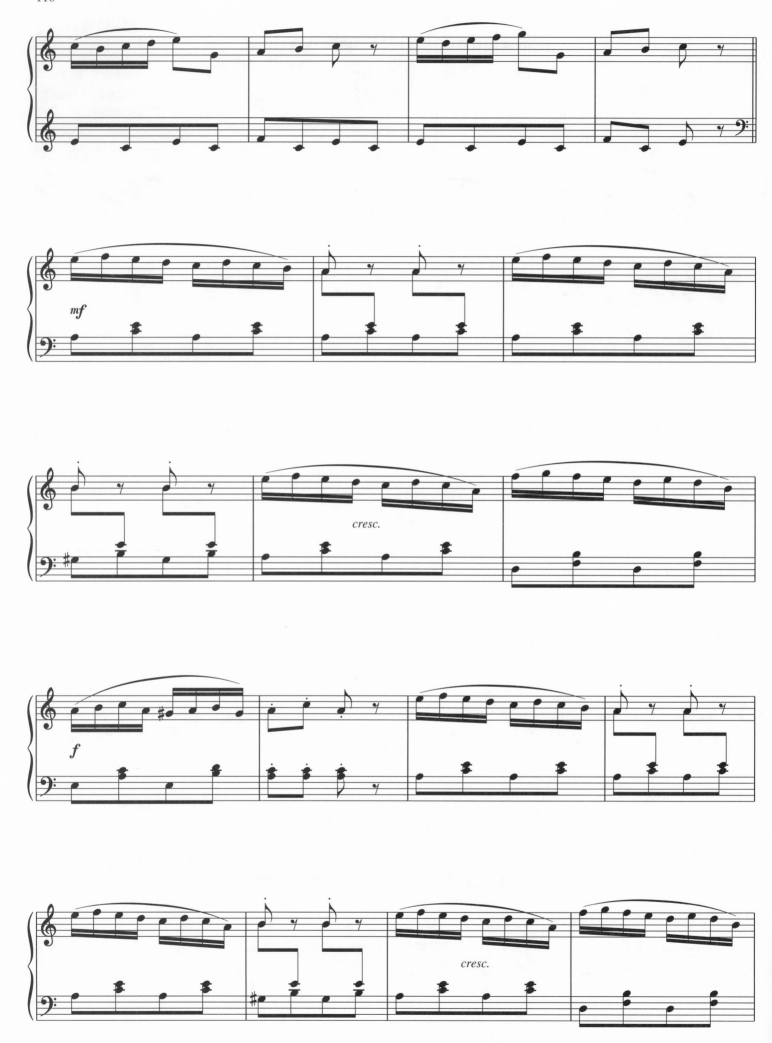

March
from ALBUMLEAVES FOR THE YOUNG

Cornelius Gurlitt
1820–1901
Op. 101, No. 1

Vivace, ma non troppo

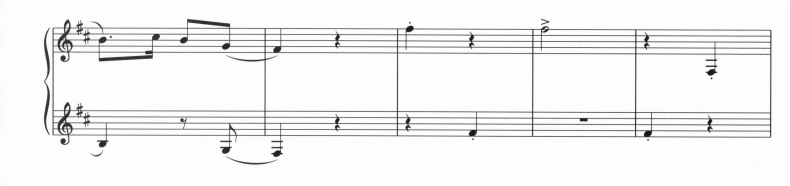

Slumber Song
from ALBUMLEAVES FOR THE YOUNG

Cornelius Gurlitt
1820–1901
Op. 101, No. 6

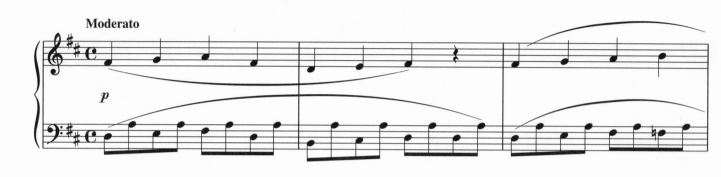

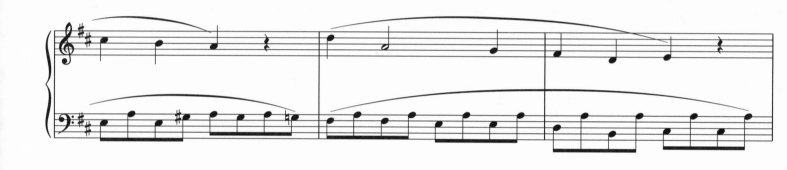

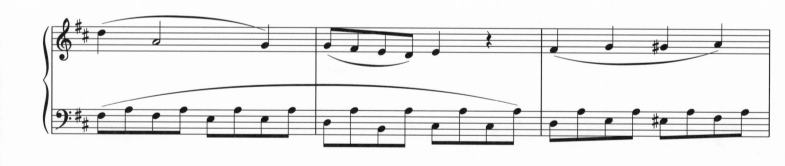

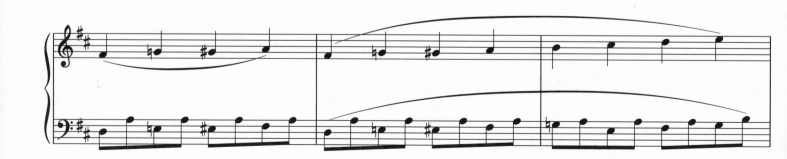

Courante

George Frideric Handel
1685–1759

Air and Variations
("The Harmonious Blacksmith")
from SUITE NO. 5

George Frideric Handel
1685–1759

Var. 1

Var. 2

Var. 3

Var. 4

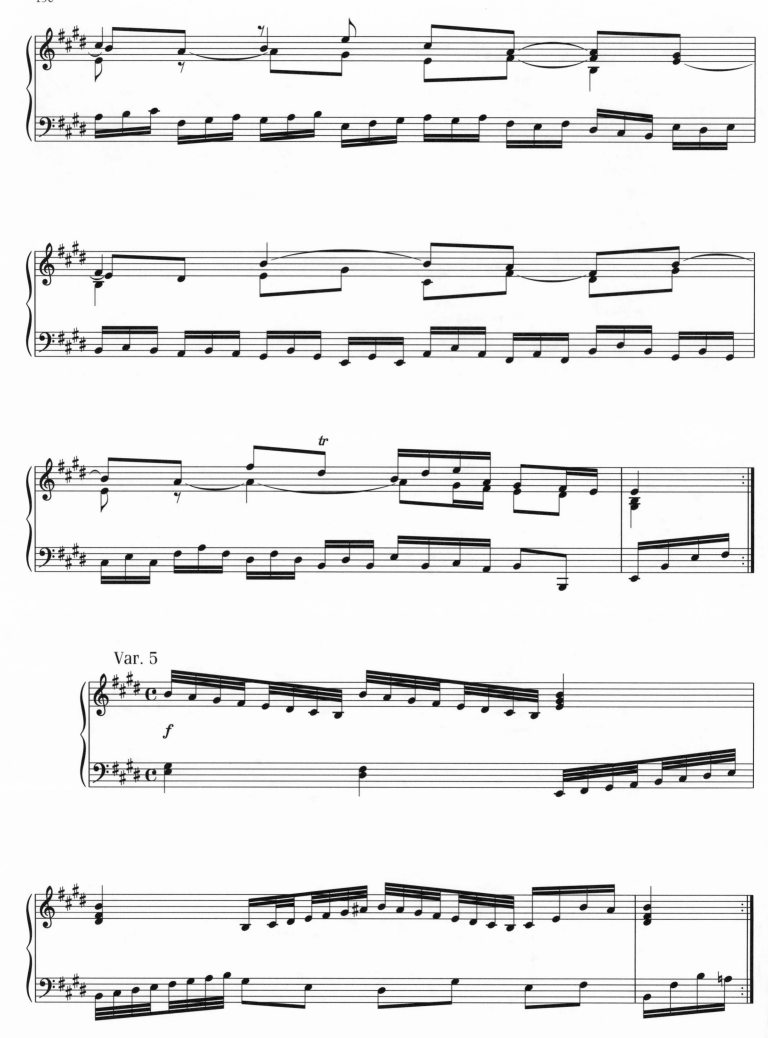

132

Rigaudon

George Frideric Handel
1685–1759

Sarabande
from SUITE NO. 11

George Frideric Handel
1685–1759

Var. 1

136

Var. 2

Country Dance

Franz Joseph Haydn
1732–1809

Allegretto

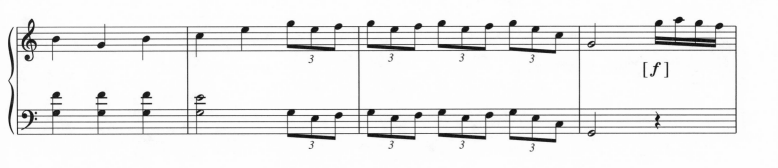

Sonata No. 1 in G Major

Franz Joseph Haydn
1732–1809
Hob. XVI/8

MENUET

Les Carillons

Johann Philipp Kirnberger
1721–1783

Fine

Alternativo

D. C. al Fine

Over Hill and Dale

Stephen Heller
1813–1888
Op. 45, No. 24

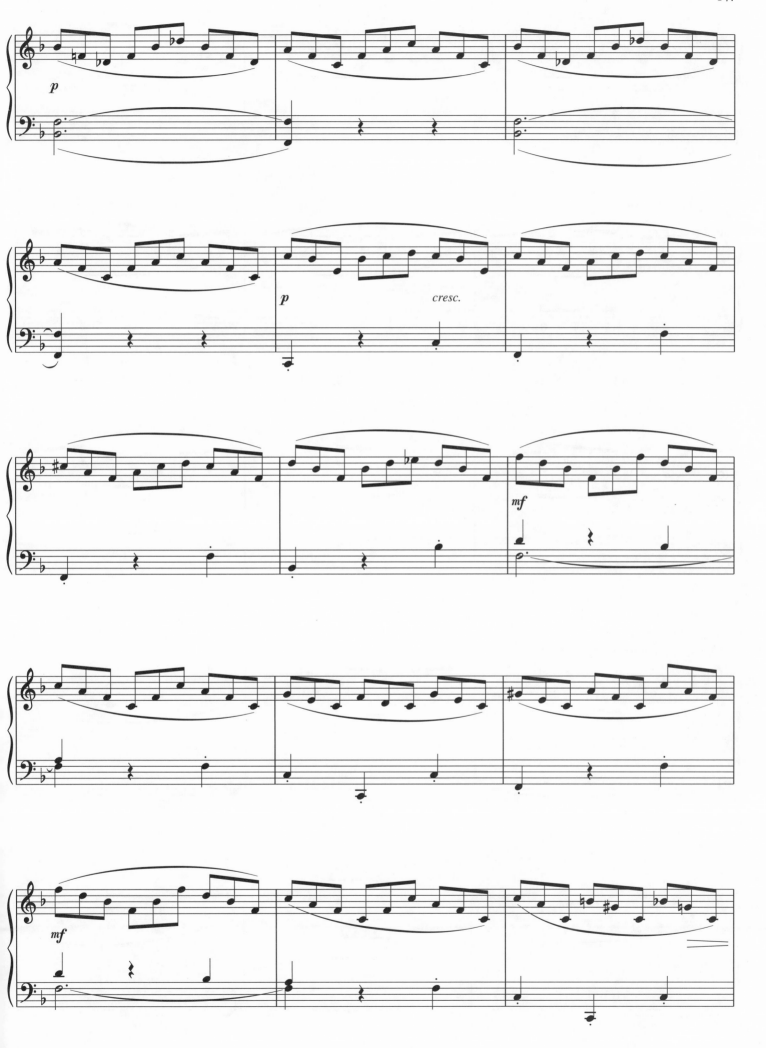

Song of May

Stephen Heller
1813–1888
Op. 45, No. 5

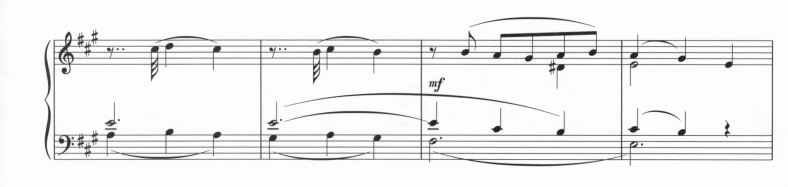

The Brook

Stephen Heller
1813–1888
Op. 45, No. 1

Allegretto

Gondola Song in A Major

Felix Mendelssohn
1809–1847
Composed 1837

Consolation

Felix Mendelssohn
1809–1841
Op. 30, No. 3

Adagio non troppo

Regrets

Felix Mendelssohn
1809–1847
Op. 19, No. 2

Venetian Boat Song No. 2

Felix Mendelssohn
1809–1847
Op. 30, No. 6

Allegretto tranquillo

168

Air in A-flat Major
from THE LONDON NOTEBOOK

Wolfgang Amadeus Mozart
1756–1791
K 109b, No. 8

Funeral March for Maestro Counterpoint

Wolfgang Amadeus Mozart
1756–1791
K 453a

K 453a

German Dance in C Major

Wolfgang Amadeus Mozart
1756–1791
K 605, No. 3

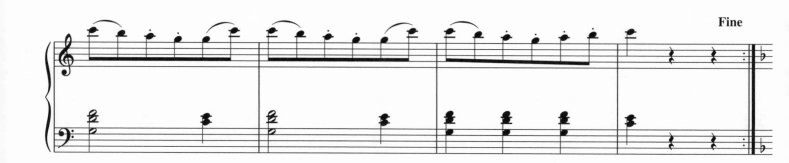

Trio (The Sleighride)

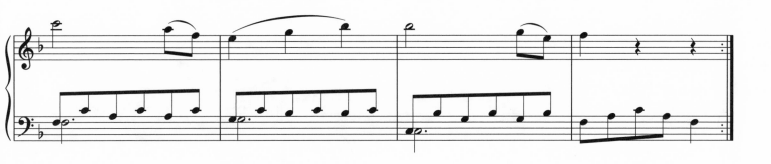

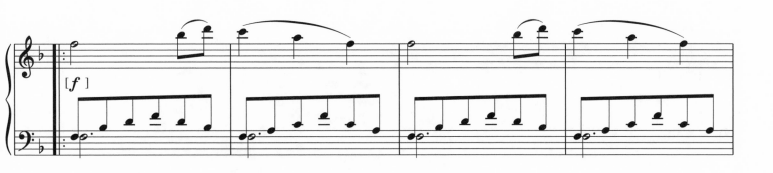

D.C. al Fine

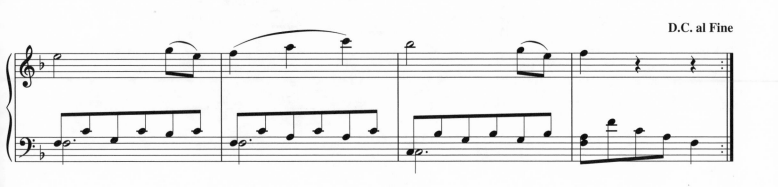

Minuet in F Major

Wolfgang Amadeus Mozart
1756–1791

[Andante]

[mf]

Little Song
from NANNERL'S NOTEBOOK

Wolfgang Amadeus Mozart
1756–1791

[Andante con moto]

Presto in B-flat Major
from THE LONDON NOTEBOOK

Wolfgang Amadeus Mozart
1756–1791
K 109b, No. 9

Rondo in C Major

Wolfgang Amadeus Mozart
1756–1791

Toccata
from SONATA IN A

Pietro Domenico Paradies [Paradisi]
1707–1791

[Allegro]

[mf]

Galop

Carl Reinecke
1824–1910

Fine

D.C. al Fine

Gavotte and Variations

Johann Pachelbel
1653–1706

Var. I

Var. II

[Andante]

Sarabande

Johann Pachelbel
1653–1706

[Andante]

[mp]

[mf]

Gymnopédie No. 1

Erik Satie
1866–1925

Lent et douloureux (slowly and mournfully)

190

Gymnopédie No. 2

Erik Satie
1866–1925

Lent et triste (slowly and sadly)

Gymnopédie No. 3

Erik Satie
1866–1925

Lent et grave (slowly and solemnly)

Sonata in D Major

Domenico Scarlatti
1685–1757
L. 263 (K. 377, P. 245)

Sonata in G Major

Domenico Scarlatti
1685–1757
L. 83 (K. 431, P. 365)

Sonata in G Major

Domenico Scarlatti
1685–1757
L. 388 (K. 2, P. 58)

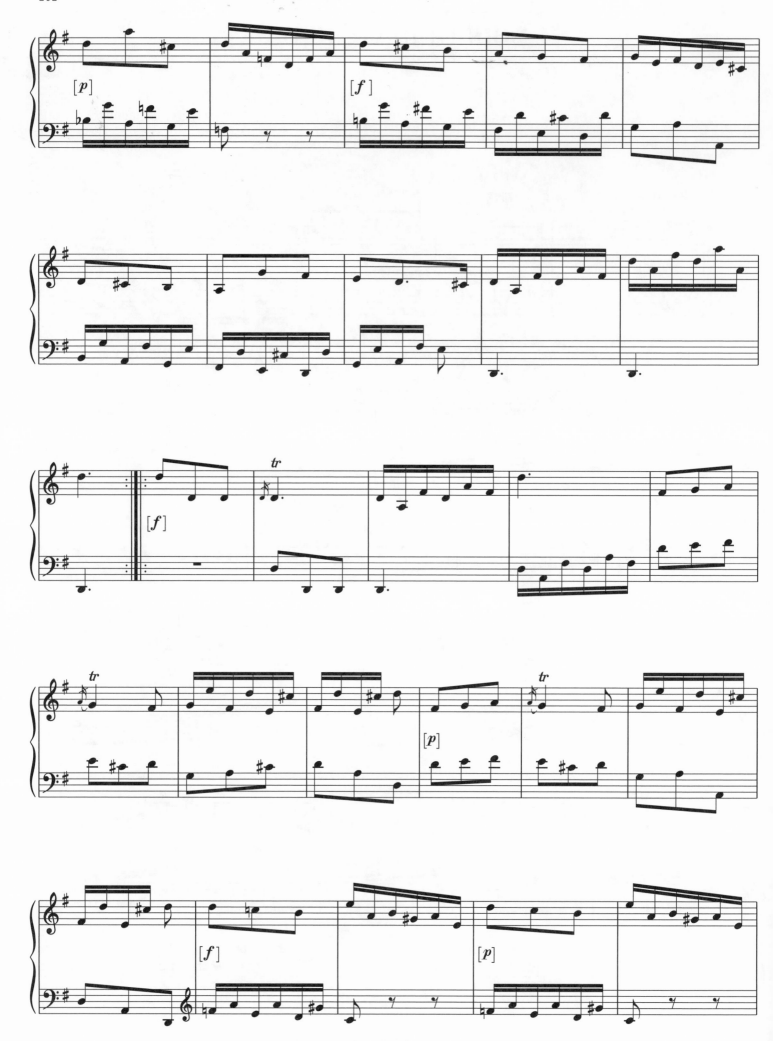

Andante in C Major

Franz Schubert
1797–1828
Composed 1812

Andante

Variation on a Waltz by Diabelli

Franz Schubert
1797–1828
Composed 1821

Waltz in A Major

Franz Schubert
1797–1828
Op. 50, No. 13

Waltz in A Minor

Franz Schubert
1797–1828
D. 969 (Op. 77, No. 9)

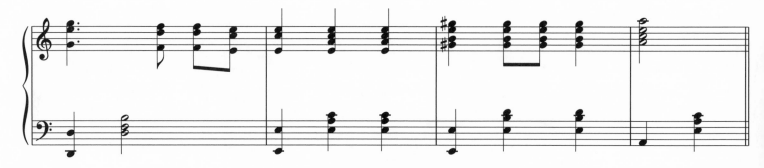

Waltz in B Minor

Franz Schubert
1797–1828
D. 145 (Op. 18a, No. 5)

[Allegro moderato]

Waltz in A-flat Major

Franz Schubert
1797–1828
Op. 33, No. 15

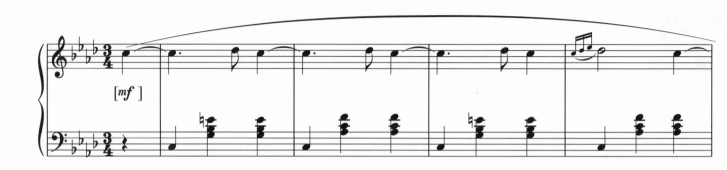

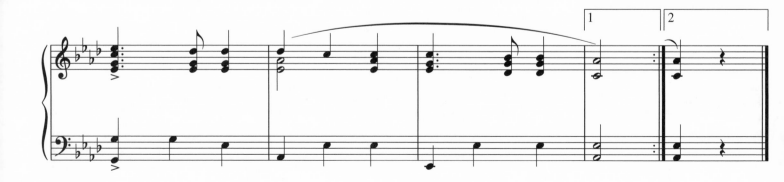

Waltz in F Minor

Franz Schubert
1797–1828
Op. 33, No. 14

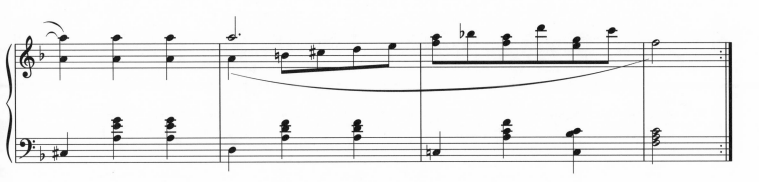

Bagatelle

Robert Schumann
1810–1856

Evensong
from SONATA IN D MAJOR

Robert Schumann
1810–1856
Op. 118b

Fantasy Dance

Robert Schumann
1810–1856
Op. 124, No. 5

Waltz

Robert Schumann
1810–1856
Op. 129, No. 4

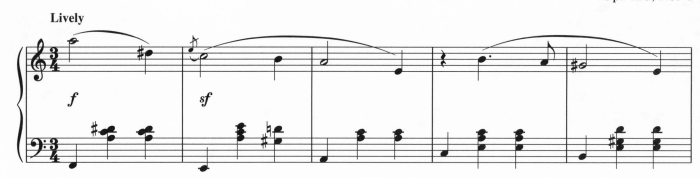

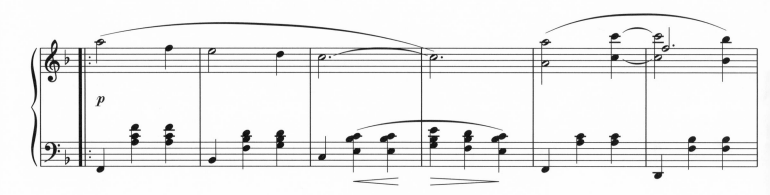

Mazurka
from ALBUM FOR THE YOUNG

Pyotr Il'yich Tchaikovsky
1840–1893
Op. 39, No. 10

227

Morning Prayer
from ALBUM FOR THE YOUNG

Pyotr Il'yich Tchaikovsky
1840–1893
Op. 39, No. 1

Waltz in E-flat Major
from ALBUM FOR THE YOUNG

Pyotr Il'yich Tchaikovsky
1840–1893
Op. 39, No. 8

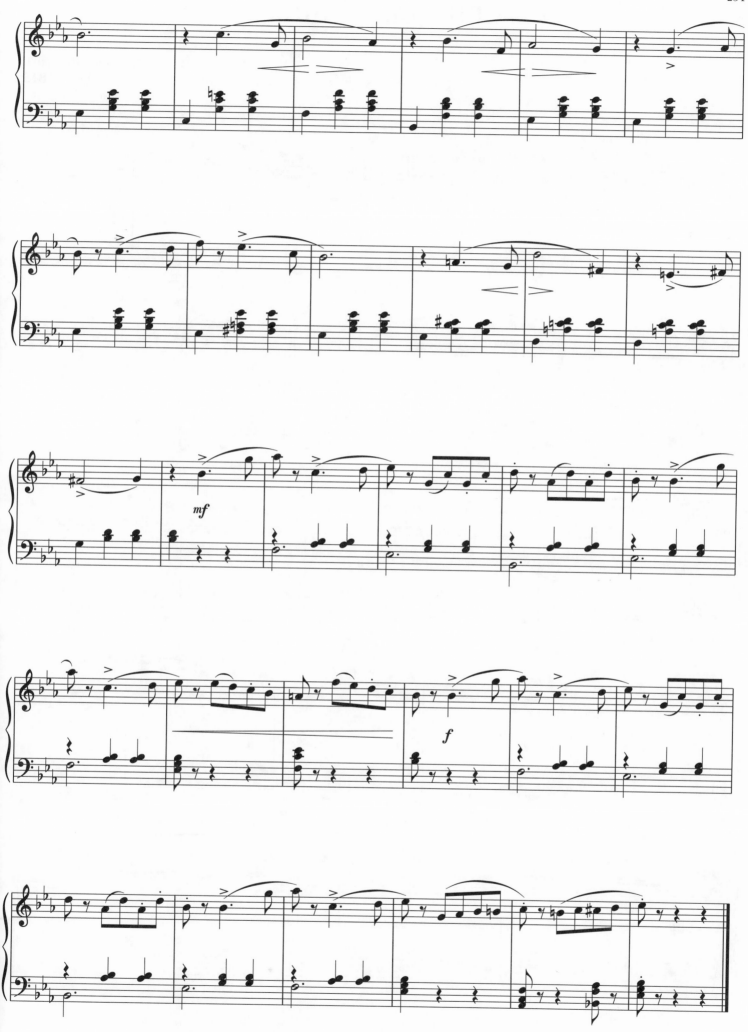

Children's Ballet

Daniel Gottlob Türk
1756–1813

The Dancing Master

Daniel Gottlob Türk
1756–1813

Allegro moderato

Sonatina in F Major

Anton Diabelli
1781–1858
Op. 168, No. 1

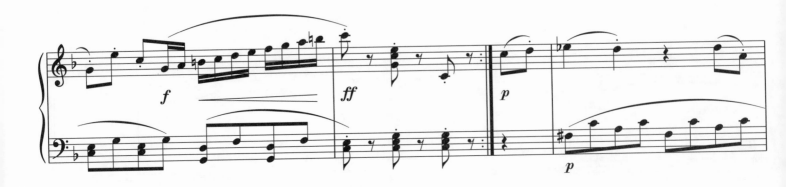

Rondo

Allegretto